THE
Prayer
MAP®

Mornings with God

BARBOUR
PUBLISHING

Scripture quotations marked NLT are taken from the *Holy Bible.* New Living Translation copyright© 1996, 2004, 2015 by Tyndale House Foundation. Used by permission of Tyndale House Publishers, Inc. Carol Stream, Illinois 60188. All rights reserved.

Scripture quotations marked MSG are from *THE MESSAGE.* Copyright © by Eugene H. Peterson 1993, 1994, 1995, 1996, 2000, 2001, 2002. Used by permission of NavPress Publishing Group.

Scripture quotations marked NIV are taken from the HOLY BIBLE, NEW INTERNATIONAL VERSION®. NIV®. Copyright © 1973, 1978, 1984, 2011 by Biblica, Inc.™ Used by permission. All rights reserved worldwide.

Published by Barbour Publishing, Inc., 1810 Barbour Drive, Uhrichsville, Ohio 44683, www.barbourbooks.com

Our mission is to inspire the world with the life-changing message of the Bible.

Printed in China.

Your Best Days Always Begin with a Prayer

Start your mornings off right with this creative journal. . .where every colorful page will guide you to create your very own inspiring prayer map—as you write out specific thoughts, ideas, and lists, which you can follow (from start to finish!) as you talk to God. (Be sure to record the date on each of your prayer maps so you can look back over time and see how God has continued to work in your life!)

The Prayer Map: Mornings with God will not only encourage you to spend your mornings in conversation with the one who loves you most. . .it will also help you build a healthy spiritual habit of continual prayer for life!

Date: ....

Good morning, God!

....
....
....
....
....

As I begin my day,
I want to share. . .

....
....
....
....
....
....
....

I am feeling. . .

....
....
....
....
....
....
....

Please infuse my
heart with Your joy!

....
....
....
....
....

Help me to accomplish. . .

Thank You for. . .

I am fully giving these worries and concerns to You. . .

Other things I need You to know, God. . .

Thank You, Father, for hearing my prayers. *Amen.*

*The faithful love of the LORD never
ends! His mercies never cease.
Great is his faithfulness; his mercies
begin afresh each morning.*
LAMENTATIONS 3:22–23 NLT

Date: ....

Good morning, God!

....
....
....
....
....

As I begin my day,
I want to share. . .

....
....
....
....
....
....
....

I am feeling. . .

....
....
....
....
....
....
....
....

Please infuse my
heart with Your joy!

....
....
....
....
....

Help me to accomplish. . .

....
....
....
....

Thank You for. . .

....
....
....
....
....
....

I am fully giving these worries and concerns to You. . .

....
....
....

Other things I need You to know, God. . .

....
....
....
....

Thank You, Father, for hearing my prayers. *Amen.*

"In the morning you will see the glory of the LORD."
EXODUS 16:7 NLT

Date: ....

Good morning, God!

....
....
....
....
....

As I begin my day,
I want to share. . .

....
....
....
....
....
....
....

I am feeling. . .

....
....
....
....
....
....
....

Please infuse my
heart with Your joy!

....
....
....
....
....

Help me to accomplish. . .

....
....
....
....

Thank You for. . .

....
....
....
....
....

I am fully giving these
worries and concerns to You. . .

....
....
....
....

Other things I need You to know, God. . .

....
....
....
....

Thank You, Father, for hearing my prayers. *Amen*.

The LORD is my shepherd, I lack nothing.
He makes me lie down in green pastures,
he leads me beside quiet waters,
he refreshes my soul.
PSALM 23:1–3 NIV

Date: ....

Good morning, God!

....
....
....
....

As I begin my day,
I want to share. . .

....
....
....
....
....
....
....

I am feeling. . .

....
....
....
....
....
....
....

Please infuse my
heart with Your joy!

....
....
....
....
....

Help me to accomplish. . .

....

....

....

....

Thank You for. . .

....

....

....

....

....

I am fully giving these
worries and concerns to You. . .

....

....

....

....

Other things I need You to know, God. . .

....

....

....

....

Thank You, Father, for hearing my prayers. *Amen*.

*I wait for the Lord more than
watchmen wait for the morning.*
PSALM 130:6 NIV

Date: ....

Good morning, God!

....
....
....
....
....

As I begin my day,
I want to share. . .

....
....
....
....
....
....
....

I am feeling. . .

....
....
....
....
....
....
....

Please infuse my
heart with Your joy!

....
....
....
....
....

Help me to accomplish. . .

....

....

....

....

Thank You for. . .

....

....

....

....

....

....

I am fully giving these
worries and concerns to You. . .

....

....

....

Other things I need You to know, God. . .

....

....

....

....

Thank You, Father, for hearing my prayers. *Amen*.

*Put GOD in charge of your work,
then what you've planned will take place.*
PROVERBS 16:3 MSG

Date: ....

Good morning, God!

....
....
....
....
....

As I begin my day,
I want to share. . .

....
....
....
....
....
....
....

I am feeling. . .

....
....
....
....
....
....
....

Please infuse my
heart with Your joy!

....
....
....
....
....

Help me to accomplish. . .

....
....
....
....

Thank You for. . .

....
....
....
....
....
....

I am fully giving these
worries and concerns to You. . .

....
....
....

Other things I need You to know, God. . .

....
....
....
....

Thank You, Father, for hearing my prayers. *Amen.*

This is the day the LORD has made.
We will rejoice and be glad in it.
PSALM 118:24 NLT

Date: ....

Good morning, God!

....

....

....

....

As I begin my day,
I want to share. . .

....

....

....

....

....

....

....

I am feeling. . .

....

....

....

....

....

....

....

Please infuse my
heart with Your joy!

....

....

....

....

....

Help me to accomplish. . .

Thank You for. . .

I am fully giving these
worries and concerns to You. . .

Other things I need You to know, God. . .

Thank You, Father, for hearing my prayers. *Amen.*

Live carefree before God; he is most careful with you.
1 PETER 5:7 MSG

Date: ....

Good morning, God!

....
....
....
....
....

As I begin my day,
I want to share. . .

....
....
....
....
....
....
....

I am feeling. . .

....
....
....
....
....
....
....

Please infuse my
heart with Your joy!

....
....
....
....
....

Help me to accomplish. . .

Thank You for. . .

I am fully giving these worries and concerns to You. . .

Other things I need You to know, God. . .

Thank You, Father, for hearing my prayers. *Amen.*

It is good to proclaim your unfailing love in the morning, your faithfulness in the evening.
PSALM 92:2 NLT

Date: ....

Good morning, God!

....
....
....
....
....

As I begin my day,
I want to share. . .

....
....
....
....
....
....
....

I am feeling. . .

....
....
....
....
....
....
....

Please infuse my
heart with Your joy!

....
....
....
....
....

Help me to accomplish. . .

_____
_____
_____
_____

Thank You for. . .

_____
_____
_____
_____
_____
_____

I am fully giving these worries and concerns to You. . .

_____
_____
_____
_____

Other things I need You to know, God. . .

_____
_____
_____
_____

Thank You, Father, for hearing my prayers. Amen.

"Seek the Kingdom of God above all else, and live righteously, and he will give you everything you need."
MATTHEW 6:33 NLT

Date: ....

Good morning, God!

....

....

....

....

....

As I begin my day,
I want to share. . .

....

....

....

....

....

....

....

I am feeling. . .

....

....

....

....

....

....

Please infuse my
heart with Your joy!

....

....

....

....

....

Help me to accomplish. . .

....

....

....

....

Thank You for. . .

....

....

....

....

....

....

I am fully giving these
worries and concerns to You. . .

....

....

....

....

Other things I need You to know, God. . .

....

....

....

....

Thank You, Father, for hearing my prayers. *Amen.*

*Let me hear of your unfailing love
each morning, for I am trusting you.
Show me where to walk, for I give myself to you.*
PSALM 143:8 NLT

Date: ....

Good morning, God!

....

....

....

....

....

As I begin my day,
I want to share. . .

I am feeling. . .

....

....

....

....

....

....

....

....

Please infuse my
heart with Your joy!

....

....

....

....

....

Help me to accomplish. . .

....
....
....
....

Thank You for. . .

....
....
....
....
....
....

I am fully giving these worries and concerns to You. . .

....
....
....
....

Other things I need You to know, God. . .

....
....
....
....

Thank You, Father, for hearing my prayers. *Amen*.

"This is my command—be strong and courageous!
Do not be afraid or discouraged. For the LORD
your God is with you wherever you go."
JOSHUA 1:9 NLT

Date: ....

Good morning, God!

....
....
....
....
....

As I begin my day,
I want to share. . .

....
....
....
....
....
....
....

I am feeling. . .

....
....
....
....
....
....
....
....

Please infuse my
heart with Your joy!

....
....
....
....
....

Help me to accomplish. . .

Thank You for. . .

I am fully giving these worries and concerns to You. . .

Other things I need You to know, God. . .

Thank You, Father, for hearing my prayers. *Amen.*

For he will command his angels concerning
you to guard you in all your ways.
PSALM 91:11 NIV

Date: ....

Good morning, God!

....
....
....
....
....

As I begin my day,
I want to share. . .

....
....
....
....
....
....
....

I am feeling. . .

....
....
....
....
....
....
....
....

Please infuse my
heart with Your joy!

....
....
....
....
....

Help me to accomplish. . .

....

....

....

....

Thank You for. . .

....

....

....

....

....

....

I am fully giving these worries and concerns to You. . .

....

....

....

....

Other things I need You to know, God. . .

....

....

....

....

Thank You, Father, for hearing my prayers. *Amen.*

*May these words of my mouth and
this meditation of my heart be pleasing in
your sight, Lord, my Rock and my Redeemer.*
PSALM 19:14 NIV

Date: ....

Good morning, God!

....
....
....
....
....

As I begin my day,
I want to share. . .

....
....
....
....
....
....
....

I am feeling. . .

....
....
....
....
....
....
....

Please infuse my
heart with Your joy!

....
....
....
....
....

Help me to accomplish. . .

....

....

....

....

Thank You for. . .

....

....

....

....

....

....

I am fully giving these
worries and concerns to You. . .

....

....

....

....

Other things I need You to know, God. . .

....

....

....

....

Thank You, Father, for hearing my prayers. *Amen.*

*Instead of worrying, pray. Let petitions and
praises shape your worries into prayers,
letting God know your concerns.*
PHILIPPIANS 4:6 MSG

Date: ....

Good morning, God!

....
....
....
....
....

As I begin my day,
I want to share. . .

....
....
....
....
....
....
....

I am feeling. . .

....
....
....
....
....
....
....

Please infuse my
heart with Your joy!

....
....
....
....
....

Help me to accomplish. . .

....
....
....
....

Thank You for. . .

....
....
....
....
....
....

I am fully giving these
worries and concerns to You. . .

....
....
....
....

Other things I need You to know, God. . .

....
....
....
....
....

Thank You, Father, for hearing my prayers. *Amen.*

Morning, noon, and night. . .
the LORD hears my voice.
PSALM 55:17 NLT

Date: ....

Good morning, God!

....
....
....
....
....

As I begin my day,
I want to share. . .

....
....
....
....
....
....
....

I am feeling. . .

....
....
....
....
....
....
....
....

Please infuse my
heart with Your joy!

....
....
....
....
....

Help me to accomplish. . .

Thank You for. . .

I am fully giving these
worries and concerns to You. . .

Other things I need You to know, God. . .

Thank You, Father, for hearing my prayers. *Amen*.

Stay wide-awake in prayer. Most of all,
love each other as if your life depended on it.
Love makes up for practically anything.
1 PETER 4:7–8 MSG

Date: ....

Good morning, God!

....
....
....
....
....

As I begin my day,
I want to share. . .

....
....
....
....
....
....
....

I am feeling. . .

....
....
....
....
....
....
....
....

Please infuse my
heart with Your joy!

....
....
....
....
....

Help me to accomplish. . .

....

....

....

....

Thank You for. . .

....

....

....

....

....

I am fully giving these worries and concerns to You. . .

....

....

....

....

Other things I need You to know, God. . .

....

....

....

....

Thank You, Father, for hearing my prayers. *Amen.*

*"You can pray for anything, and if
you have faith, you will receive it."*
MATTHEW 21:22 NLT

Date: ....

Good morning, God!

....
....
....
....
....

As I begin my day,
I want to share. . .

....
....
....
....
....
....
....

I am feeling. . .

....
....
....
....
....
....
....
....

Please infuse my
heart with Your joy!

....
....
....
....
....

Help me to accomplish. . .

....

....

....

....

Thank You for. . .

....

....

....

....

....

I am fully giving these worries and concerns to You. . .

....

....

....

Other things I need You to know, God. . .

....

....

....

....

Thank You, Father, for hearing my prayers. Amen.

If any of you lacks wisdom, you should ask God, who gives generously to all without finding fault, and it will be given to you.
JAMES 1:5 NIV

Date: ....

Good morning, God!

....
....
....
....
....

As I begin my day,
I want to share. . .

....
....
....
....
....
....
....

I am feeling. . .

....
....
....
....
....
....
....
....

Please infuse my
heart with Your joy!

....
....
....
....
....

Help me to accomplish. . .

....

....

....

....

Thank You for. . .

....

....

....

....

....

....

I am fully giving these
worries and concerns to You. . .

....

....

....

....

Other things I need You to know, God. . .

....

....

....

....

Thank You, Father, for hearing my prayers. *Amen.*

And it is impossible to please God without faith.
Anyone who wants to come to him must believe that God
exists and that he rewards those who sincerely seek him.
HEBREWS 11:6 NLT

Date: ....

Good morning, God!

....

....

....

....

....

As I begin my day,
I want to share. . .

....

....

....

....

....

....

....

I am feeling. . .

....

....

....

....

....

....

....

....

Please infuse my
heart with Your joy!

....

....

....

....

....

Help me to accomplish. . .

....

....

....

....

Thank You for. . .

....

....

....

....

....

....

I am fully giving these worries and concerns to You. . .

....

....

....

Other things I need You to know, God. . .

....

....

....

....

Thank You, Father, for hearing my prayers. *Amen.*

*"Truly I tell you, if you have faith as small as a
mustard seed, you can say to this mountain,
'Move from here to there,' and it will move.
Nothing will be impossible for you."*
MATTHEW 17:20 NIV

Date: ....

Good morning, God!

....
....
....
....

As I begin my day,
I want to share. . .

....
....
....
....
....
....
....

I am feeling. . .

....
....
....
....
....
....
....

Please infuse my
heart with Your joy!

....
....
....
....
....

Help me to accomplish. . .

Thank You for. . .

I am fully giving these worries and concerns to You. . .

Other things I need You to know, God. . .

Thank You, Father, for hearing my prayers. *Amen.*

Blessed be God—he heard me praying. He proved he's on my side; I've thrown my lot in with him.
PSALM 28:6 MSG

Date: ....

Good morning, God!

....

....

....

....

As I begin my day,
I want to share. . .

....

....

....

....

....

....

....

I am feeling. . .

....

....

....

....

....

....

....

Please infuse my
heart with Your joy!

....

....

....

....

....

Help me to accomplish. . .

....

....

....

....

Thank You for. . .

....

....

....

....

....

I am fully giving these
worries and concerns to You. . .

....

....

....

Other things I need You to know, God. . .

....

....

....

....

Thank You, Father, for hearing my prayers. *Amen.*

Listen to my voice in the morning, LORD.
Each morning I bring my requests
to you and wait expectantly.
PSALM 5:3 NLT

Date: ....

Good morning, God!

....

....

....

....

....

As I begin my day,
I want to share. . .

....

....

....

....

....

....

....

....

I am feeling. . .

....

....

....

....

....

....

....

Please infuse my
heart with Your joy!

....

....

....

....

....

Help me to accomplish. . .

....

....

....

....

Thank You for. . .

....

....

....

....

....

I am fully giving these worries and concerns to You. . .

....

....

....

Other things I need You to know, God. . .

....

....

....

....

Thank You, Father, for hearing my prayers. *Amen.*

Let every living, breathing creature praise GOD!
PSALM 150:6 MSG

Date: ....

Good morning, God!

....
....
....
....
....

As I begin my day,
I want to share. . .

....
....
....
....
....
....
....

I am feeling. . .

....
....
....
....
....
....
....

Please infuse my
heart with Your joy!

....
....
....
....
....

Help me to accomplish. . .

Thank You for. . .

I am fully giving these worries and concerns to You. . .

Other things I need You to know, God. . .

Thank You, Father, for hearing my prayers. *Amen.*

Because your love is better than life, my lips will glorify you. I will praise you as long as I live, and in your name I will lift up my hands.
PSALM 63:3–4 NIV

Date: ....

Good morning, God!

....
....
....
....
....

As I begin my day,
I want to share. . .

....
....
....
....
....
....
....

I am feeling. . .

....
....
....
....
....
....
....
....
....

Please infuse my
heart with Your joy!

....
....
....
....
....
....

Help me to accomplish. . .

....
....
....
....

Thank You for. . .

....
....
....
....
....
....

I am fully giving these
worries and concerns to You. . .

....
....
....
....

Other things I need You to know, God. . .

....
....
....
....

Thank You, Father, for hearing my prayers. *Amen.*

Look to the LORD and his strength; seek his face always.
1 CHRONICLES 16:11 NIV

Date: ....

Good morning, God!

....
....
....
....
....

As I begin my day,
I want to share. . .

....
....
....
....
....
....
....

I am feeling. . .

....
....
....
....
....
....
....
....

Please infuse my
heart with Your joy!

....
....
....
....
....
....

Help me to accomplish. . .

....

....

....

....

Thank You for. . .

....

....

....

....

....

....

I am fully giving these
worries and concerns to You. . .

....

....

....

....

Other things I need You to know, God. . .

....

....

....

....

Thank You, Father, for hearing my prayers. *Amen.*

*For great is your love toward me;
you have delivered me from the depths.*
PSALM 86:13 NIV

Date: ....

Good morning, God!

....
....
....
....
....

As I begin my day,
I want to share. . .

....
....
....
....
....
....
....

I am feeling. . .

....
....
....
....
....
....
....
....

Please infuse my
heart with Your joy!

....
....
....
....
....

Help me to accomplish. . .

Thank You for. . .

I am fully giving these
worries and concerns to You. . .

Other things I need You to know, God. . .

Thank You, Father, for hearing my prayers. *Amen.*

*"But blessed is the one who trusts in
the LORD, whose confidence is in him."*
JEREMIAH 17:7 NIV

Date: ....

Good morning, God!

....
....
....
....
....

As I begin my day,
I want to share. . .

....
....
....
....
....
....
....

I am feeling. . .

....
....
....
....
....
....
....
....

Please infuse my
heart with Your joy!

....
....
....
....
....
....

Help me to accomplish. . .

....
....
....
....

Thank You for. . .

....
....
....
....
....
....

I am fully giving these
worries and concerns to You. . .

....
....
....
....

Other things I need You to know, God. . .

....
....
....
....

Thank You, Father, for hearing my prayers. *Amen.*

*Each morning I will sing with joy about your
unfailing love. For you have been my refuge,
a place of safety when I am in distress.*
PSALM 59:16 NLT

Date: ....

Good morning, God!

....

....

....

....

As I begin my day,
I want to share. . .

....

....

....

....

....

....

....

I am feeling. . .

....

....

....

....

....

....

Please infuse my
heart with Your joy!

....

....

....

....

....

Help me to accomplish. . .

Thank You for. . .

I am fully giving these worries and concerns to You. . .

Other things I need You to know, God. . .

Thank You, Father, for hearing my prayers. *Amen.*

Trust GOD from the bottom of your heart; don't try to figure out everything on your own. Listen for GOD's voice in everything you do, everywhere you go; he's the one who will keep you on track.

PROVERBS 3:5–6 MSG

Date: ....

Good morning, God!

....
....
....
....
....

As I begin my day,
I want to share. . .

....
....
....
....
....
....
....

I am feeling. . .

....
....
....
....
....
....
....
....

Please infuse my
heart with Your joy!

....
....
....
....
....

Help me to accomplish. . .

....

....

....

....

Thank You for. . .

....

....

....

....

....

I am fully giving these
worries and concerns to You. . .

....

....

....

Other things I need You to know, God. . .

....

....

....

....

Thank You, Father, for hearing my prayers. *Amen.*

*O LORD, I cry out to you. I will
keep on pleading day by day.*
PSALM 88:13 NLT

Date: ....

Good morning, God!
....
....
....
....

As I begin my day,
I want to share. . .
....
....
....
....
....
....
....

I am feeling. . .
....
....
....
....
....
....
....
....

Please infuse my
heart with Your joy!
....
....
....
....
....

Help me to accomplish. . .

_____
_____
_____
_____

Thank You for. . .

_____
_____
_____
_____
_____

I am fully giving these
worries and concerns to You. . .

_____
_____
_____
_____

Other things I need You to know, God. . .

_____
_____
_____
_____

Thank You, Father, for hearing my prayers. *Amen.*

God, make a fresh start in me.
PSALM 51:10 MSG

Date: ....

Good morning, God!

....
....
....
....
....

As I begin my day,
I want to share. . .

....
....
....
....
....
....
....

I am feeling. . .

....
....
....
....
....
....
....

Please infuse my
heart with Your joy!

....
....
....
....
....

Help me to accomplish. . .

....

....

....

....

Thank You for. . .

....

....

....

....

....

....

I am fully giving these
worries and concerns to You. . .

....

....

....

....

Other things I need You to know, God. . .

....

....

....

....

Thank You, Father, for hearing my prayers. *Amen.*

*Praise the LORD, my soul; all my inmost being,
praise his holy name. Praise the LORD, my soul,
and forget not all his benefits—who forgives all your
sins and heals all your diseases, who redeems your life
from the pit and crowns you with love and compassion.*
PSALM 103:1–4 NIV

Date: ....

Good morning, God!

....
....
....
....
....

As I begin my day,
I want to share. . .

....
....
....
....
....
....
....
....

I am feeling. . .

....
....
....
....
....
....
....
....

Please infuse my
heart with Your joy!

....
....
....
....
....

Help me to accomplish. . .

....
....
....
....

Thank You for. . .

....
....
....
....
....
....

I am fully giving these
worries and concerns to You. . .

....
....
....

Other things I need You to know, God. . .

....
....
....
....

Thank You, Father, for hearing my prayers. *Amen*.

Weeping may last through the night,
but joy comes with the morning.
PSALM 30:5 NLT

Date: ....

Good morning, God!

....
....
....
....
....

As I begin my day,
I want to share. . .

....
....
....
....
....
....
....

I am feeling. . .

....
....
....
....
....
....
....

Please infuse my
heart with Your joy!

....
....
....
....
....

Help me to accomplish. . .

Thank You for. . .

I am fully giving these worries and concerns to You. . .

Other things I need You to know, God. . .

Thank You, Father, for hearing my prayers. *Amen.*

The wise counsel God gives when I'm awake is confirmed by my sleeping heart. Day and night I'll stick with God; I've got a good thing going and I'm not letting go.
PSALM 16:7–8 MSG

Date: ....

Good morning, God!

....
....
....
....
....

As I begin my day,
I want to share. . .

....
....
....
....
....
....
....

I am feeling. . .

....
....
....
....
....
....
....

Please infuse my
heart with Your joy!

....
....
....
....
....

Help me to accomplish. . .

....

....

....

....

Thank You for. . .

....

....

....

....

....

I am fully giving these worries and concerns to You. . .

....

....

....

Other things I need You to know, God. . .

....

....

....

....

Thank You, Father, for hearing my prayers. Amen.

I'm ready, God, so ready, ready from head to toe, ready to sing, ready to raise a tune: "Wake up, soul! Wake up, harp! wake up, lute! Wake up, you sleepyhead sun!"

PSALM 57:7–8 MSG

Date: ....

Good morning, God!

....
....
....
....
....

As I begin my day,
I want to share. . .

....
....
....
....
....
....
....

I am feeling. . .

....
....
....
....
....
....
....
....
....

Please infuse my
heart with Your joy!

....
....
....
....
....
....

Help me to accomplish. . .

Thank You for. . .

I am fully giving these
worries and concerns to You. . .

Other things I need You to know, God. . .

Thank You, Father, for hearing my prayers. *Amen.*

*Hurry with your answer, GOD! . . . Don't turn away;
don't ignore me! . . . If you wake me each
morning with the sound of your loving voice,
I'll go to sleep each night trusting in you.*
PSALM 143:7–8 MSG

Date: ....

Good morning, God!

....
....
....
....
....

As I begin my day,
I want to share. . .

....
....
....
....
....
....
....

I am feeling. . .

....
....
....
....
....
....
....

Please infuse my
heart with Your joy!

....
....
....
....
....

Help me to accomplish. . .

....
....
....
....
....

Thank You for. . .

....
....
....
....
....
....

I am fully giving these
worries and concerns to You. . .

....
....
....
....

Other things I need You to know, God. . .

....
....
....
....

Thank You, Father, for hearing my prayers. *Amen.*

*Be careful how you live. Don't live like fools,
but like those who are wise. Make the most
of every opportunity in these evil days.*
EPHESIANS 5:15–16 NLT

Date: ....

Good morning, God!

....
....
....
....

As I begin my day,
I want to share. . .

....
....
....
....
....
....
....

I am feeling. . .

....
....
....
....
....
....
....

Please infuse my
heart with Your joy!

....
....
....
....
....

Help me to accomplish. . .

....

....

....

....

Thank You for. . .

....

....

....

....

....

I am fully giving these worries and concerns to You. . .

....

....

....

....

Other things I need You to know, God. . .

....

....

....

....

Thank You, Father, for hearing my prayers. *Amen.*

Because I am righteous, I will see you. When I awake,
I will see you face to face and be satisfied.
PSALM 17:15 NLT

Date: ....

Good morning, God!

....
....
....
....
....

As I begin my day,
I want to share. . .

....
....
....
....
....
....
....

I am feeling. . .

....
....
....
....
....
....
....

Please infuse my
heart with Your joy!

....
....
....
....
....

Help me to accomplish. . .

....

....

....

....

Thank You for. . .

....

....

....

....

....

....

I am fully giving these worries and concerns to You. . .

....

....

....

....

Other things I need You to know, God. . .

....

....

....

....

Thank You, Father, for hearing my prayers. *Amen*.

The Sovereign LORD has given me his words of wisdom, so that I know how to comfort the weary. Morning by morning he wakens me and opens my understanding to his will.
ISAIAH 50:4 NLT

Date: ....

Good morning, God!

....

....

....

....

....

As I begin my day,
I want to share. . .

....

....

....

....

....

....

....

I am feeling. . .

....

....

....

....

....

....

....

....

Please infuse my
heart with Your joy!

....

....

....

....

....

....

Help me to accomplish. . .

....

....

....

....

Thank You for. . .

....

....

....

....

....

....

I am fully giving these
worries and concerns to You. . .

....

....

....

....

Other things I need You to know, God. . .

....

....

....

....

Thank You, Father, for hearing my prayers. *Amen.*

*"Awake, O sleeper, rise up from the dead,
and Christ will give you light."*
EPHESIANS 5:14 NLT

Date: ....

Good morning, God!

....

....

....

....

....

As I begin my day,
I want to share. . .

....

....

....

....

....

....

....

I am feeling. . .

....

....

....

....

....

....

....

Please infuse my
heart with Your joy!

....

....

....

....

....

Help me to accomplish. . .

....

....

....

....

Thank You for. . .

....

....

....

....

....

....

I am fully giving these worries and concerns to You. . .

....

....

....

....

Other things I need You to know, God. . .

....

....

....

....

Thank You, Father, for hearing my prayers. *Amen*.

God remains the strength of my heart; he is mine forever.
PSALM 73:26 NLT

Date: ....

Good morning, God!

....
....
....
....
....

As I begin my day,
I want to share. . .

....
....
....
....
....
....
....

I am feeling. . .

....
....
....
....
....
....
....

Please infuse my
heart with Your joy!

....
....
....
....
....

Help me to accomplish. . .

Thank You for. . .

I am fully giving these worries and concerns to You. . .

Other things I need You to know, God. . .

Thank You, Father, for hearing my prayers. *Amen.*

By your words I can see where I'm going;
they throw a beam of light on my dark path.
PSALM 119:105 MSG

Date: ....

Good morning, God!

....
....
....
....
....

As I begin my day,
I want to share. . .

....
....
....
....
....
....
....

I am feeling. . .

....
....
....
....
....
....
....
....

Please infuse my
heart with Your joy!

....
....
....
....
....

Help me to accomplish. . .

....

....

....

....

Thank You for. . .

....

....

....

....

....

I am fully giving these worries and concerns to You. . .

....

....

....

....

Other things I need You to know, God. . .

....

....

....

....

Thank You, Father, for hearing my prayers. *Amen.*

The fundamental fact of existence is that this trust in God, this faith, is the firm foundation under everything that makes life worth living. It's our handle on what we can't see.
HEBREWS 11:1 MSG

Date: ....

Good morning, God!

....
....
....
....
....

As I begin my day,
I want to share. . .

....
....
....
....
....
....
....

I am feeling. . .

....
....
....
....
....
....
....
....

Please infuse my
heart with Your joy!

....
....
....
....
....

Help me to accomplish. . .

....

....

....

....

Thank You for. . .

....

....

....

....

....

I am fully giving these
worries and concerns to You. . .

....

....

....

Other things I need You to know, God. . .

....

....

....

....

Thank You, Father, for hearing my prayers. *Amen*.

I pray to God—my life a prayer—
and wait for what he'll say and do.
PSALM 130:5 MSG

Date: ....

Good morning, God!

....
....
....
....
....

As I begin my day,
I want to share. . .

....
....
....
....
....
....
....
....

I am feeling. . .

....
....
....
....
....
....
....
....
....

Please infuse my
heart with Your joy!

....
....
....
....
....

Help me to accomplish. . .

Thank You for. . .

I am fully giving these
worries and concerns to You. . .

Other things I need You to know, God. . .

Thank You, Father, for hearing my prayers. *Amen.*

Yes, my soul, find rest in God;
my hope comes from him.
PSALM 62:5 NIV

Date: ....

Good morning, God!

....

....

....

....

As I begin my day,
I want to share. . .

....

....

....

....

....

....

....

I am feeling. . .

....

....

....

....

....

....

....

Please infuse my
heart with Your joy!

....

....

....

....

....

Help me to accomplish. . .

Thank You for. . .

I am fully giving these worries and concerns to You. . .

Other things I need You to know, God. . .

Thank You, Father, for hearing my prayers. *Amen.*

For the LORD has told me this: "I will watch quietly from my dwelling place—as quietly as the heat rises on a summer day, or as the morning dew forms during the harvest."

ISAIAH 18:4 NLT

Date: ....

Good morning, God!

....
....
....
....
....

As I begin my day,
I want to share. . .

....
....
....
....
....
....
....

I am feeling. . .

....
....
....
....
....
....
....

Please infuse my
heart with Your joy!

....
....
....
....
....

Help me to accomplish. . .

....

....

....

....

Thank You for. . .

....

....

....

....

....

I am fully giving these
worries and concerns to You. . .

....

....

....

Other things I need You to know, God. . .

....

....

....

....

Thank You, Father, for hearing my prayers. *Amen.*

*"Stop at the crossroads and look around.
Ask for the old, godly way, and walk in it.
Travel its path, and you will find rest for your souls."*
JEREMIAH 6:16 NLT

Date: ....

Good morning, God!

....
....
....
....
....

As I begin my day,
I want to share. . .

....
....
....
....
....
....
....

I am feeling. . .

....
....
....
....
....
....
....
....
....

Please infuse my
heart with Your joy!

....
....
....
....
....

Help me to accomplish. . .

....

....

....

....

Thank You for. . .

....

....

....

....

....

I am fully giving these worries and concerns to You. . .

....

....

....

....

Other things I need You to know, God. . .

....

....

....

....

Thank You, Father, for hearing my prayers. *Amen.*

*[Jesus said,] "I came so they can have real and eternal life,
more and better life than they ever dreamed of."*
JOHN 10:10 MSG

Date: ....

Good morning, God!

....
....
....
....
....

As I begin my day,
I want to share. . .

....
....
....
....
....
....
....

I am feeling. . .

....
....
....
....
....
....
....

Please infuse my
heart with Your joy!

....
....
....
....
....

Help me to accomplish. . .

....
....
....

Thank You for. . .

....
....
....
....
....

I am fully giving these
worries and concerns to You. . .

....
....
....
....

Other things I need You to know, God. . .

....
....
....
....

Thank You, Father, for hearing my prayers. *Amen.*

*"You will seek me and find me when
you seek me with all your heart."*
JEREMIAH 29:13 NIV

Date: ....

Good morning, God!

....
....
....
....
....

As I begin my day,
I want to share. . .

....
....
....
....
....
....
....

I am feeling. . .

....
....
....
....
....
....
....
....

Please infuse my
heart with Your joy!

....
....
....
....
....
....

Help me to accomplish. . .

....

....

....

....

Thank You for. . .

....

....

....

....

....

....

I am fully giving these worries and concerns to You. . .

....

....

....

....

Other things I need You to know, God. . .

....

....

....

....

Thank You, Father, for hearing my prayers. *Amen.*

One thing I ask from the LORD, this only do I seek: that I may dwell in the house of the LORD all the days of my life.
PSALM 27:4 NIV

Date: ....

Good morning, God!

....
....
....
....
....

As I begin my day,
I want to share. . .

....
....
....
....
....
....
....

I am feeling. . .

....
....
....
....
....
....
....
....

Please infuse my
heart with Your joy!

....
....
....
....
....
....

Help me to accomplish. . .

....
....
....
....

Thank You for. . .

....
....
....
....
....
....

I am fully giving these worries and concerns to You. . .

....
....
....
....

Other things I need You to know, God. . .

....
....
....
....

Thank You, Father, for hearing my prayers. *Amen.*

You will keep in perfect peace those whose minds are steadfast, because they trust in you.
Isaiah 26:3 niv

Date: ....

Good morning, God!

....
....
....
....
....

As I begin my day,
I want to share. . .

....
....
....
....
....
....
....
....

I am feeling. . .

....
....
....
....
....
....
....
....
....

Please infuse my
heart with Your joy!

....
....
....
....
....

Help me to accomplish. . .

Thank You for. . .

I am fully giving these
worries and concerns to You. . .

Other things I need You to know, God. . .

Thank You, Father, for hearing my prayers. *Amen.*

It is the LORD who created the stars, the Pleiades and Orion.
He turns darkness into morning and day into night.
AMOS 5:8 NLT

Date: ....

Good morning, God!

....

....

....

....

....

As I begin my day,
I want to share. . .

....

....

....

....

....

....

....

I am feeling. . .

....

....

....

....

....

....

....

....

Please infuse my
heart with Your joy!

....

....

....

....

....

....

Help me to accomplish. . .

....
....
....
....

Thank You for. . .

....
....
....
....
....
....

I am fully giving these
worries and concerns to You. . .

....
....
....
....

Other things I need You to know, God. . .

....
....
....
....

Thank You, Father, for hearing my prayers. *Amen.*

*God rewrote the text of my life when I
opened the book of my heart to his eyes.*
PSALM 18:24 MSG

Date: ....

Good morning, God!
....
....
....
....
....

As I begin my day,
I want to share. . .
....
....
....
....
....
....
....

I am feeling. . .
....
....
....
....
....
....
....

Please infuse my
heart with Your joy!
....
....
....
....
....

Help me to accomplish. . .

....

....

....

....

Thank You for. . .

....

....

....

....

....

....

I am fully giving these
worries and concerns to You. . .

....

....

....

....

Other things I need You to know, God. . .

....

....

....

....

Thank You, Father, for hearing my prayers. *Amen*.

*We throw open our doors to God and discover at the
same moment that he has already thrown open his door
to us. We find ourselves standing where we always hoped
we might stand—out in the wide open spaces of God's
grace and glory, standing tall and shouting our praise.*
ROMANS 5:2 MSG

Date: ....

Good morning, God!

....
....
....
....
....

As I begin my day,
I want to share. . .

....
....
....
....
....
....
....

I am feeling. . .

....
....
....
....
....
....
....
....
....

Please infuse my
heart with Your joy!

....
....
....
....
....

Help me to accomplish. . .

....

....

....

....

Thank You for. . .

....

....

....

....

....

....

I am fully giving these
worries and concerns to You. . .

....

....

....

....

Other things I need You to know, God. . .

....

....

....

....

Thank You, Father, for hearing my prayers. *Amen.*

*Now all glory to God, who is able to make
you strong, just as my Good News says.*
ROMANS 16:25 NLT

Date: ....

Good morning, God!

....
....
....
....
....

As I begin my day, I want to share. . .

....
....
....
....
....
....
....

I am feeling. . .

....
....
....
....
....
....
....

Please infuse my heart with Your joy!

....
....
....
....
....

Help me to accomplish. . .

....

....

....

....

Thank You for. . .

....

....

....

....

....

....

I am fully giving these
worries and concerns to You. . .

....

....

....

Other things I need You to know, God. . .

....

....

....

....

Thank You, Father, for hearing my prayers. *Amen*.

*God, investigate my life; get all the facts firsthand.
I'm an open book to you; even from a distance,
you know what I'm thinking. You know when I leave
and when I get back; I'm never out of your sight.*

PSALM 139:1–2 MSG

Date: ....

Good morning, God!

....
....
....
....
....

As I begin my day,
I want to share. . .

....
....
....
....
....
....
....

I am feeling. . .

....
....
....
....
....
....
....
....

Please infuse my
heart with Your joy!

....
....
....
....
....

Help me to accomplish. . .

Thank You for. . .

I am fully giving these worries and concerns to You. . .

Other things I need You to know, God. . .

Thank You, Father, for hearing my prayers. *Amen*.

God made my life complete when I placed all the pieces before him. When I cleaned up my act, he gave me a fresh start.

2 SAMUEL 22:21 MSG

Date: ....

Good morning, God!

....
....
....
....
....

As I begin my day,
I want to share. . .

....
....
....
....
....
....
....

I am feeling. . .

....
....
....
....
....
....
....

Please infuse my
heart with Your joy!

....
....
....
....
....
....

Help me to accomplish. . .

Thank You for. . .

I am fully giving these worries and concerns to You. . .

Other things I need You to know, God. . .

Thank You, Father, for hearing my prayers. *Amen.*

*GOD, come close. Come quickly! Open your ears—
it's my voice you're hearing! Treat my
prayer as sweet incense rising.*
PSALM 141:1–2 MSG

Date: ....

Good morning, God!

....
....
....
....
....

As I begin my day, I want to share. . .

....
....
....
....
....
....
....

I am feeling. . .

....
....
....
....
....
....
....
....

Please infuse my heart with Your joy!

....
....
....
....
....

Help me to accomplish. . .

....

....

....

....

Thank You for. . .

....

....

....

....

....

....

I am fully giving these
worries and concerns to You. . .

....

....

....

....

Other things I need You to know, God. . .

....

....

....

....

....

Thank You, Father, for hearing my prayers. Amen.

*In the night I search for you; in the
morning I earnestly seek you.*
ISAIAH 26:9 NLT

Date: ....

Good morning, God!

....
....
....
....
....

As I begin my day,
I want to share. . .

....
....
....
....
....
....

I am feeling. . .

....
....
....
....
....
....

Please infuse my
heart with Your joy!

....
....
....
....
....

Help me to accomplish. . .

Thank You for. . .

I am fully giving these worries and concerns to You. . .

Other things I need You to know, God. . .

Thank You, Father, for hearing my prayers. Amen.

Clean the slate, God, so we can start the day fresh!
Keep me from stupid sins, from thinking I can
take over your work; then I can start this day
sun-washed, scrubbed clean of the grime of sin.
PSALM 19:12–13 MSG

Date: ....

Good morning, God!

....

....

....

....

....

As I begin my day,
I want to share. . .

....

....

....

....

....

....

....

I am feeling. . .

....

....

....

....

....

....

....

Please infuse my
heart with Your joy!

....

....

....

....

....

Help me to accomplish. . .

Thank You for. . .

I am fully giving these worries and concerns to You. . .

Other things I need You to know, God. . .

Thank You, Father, for hearing my prayers. *Amen.*

Open your ears, God, to my prayer; don't pretend you don't hear me knocking. Come close and whisper your answer. I really need you.
PSALM 55:1–2 MSG

Date: ....

Good morning, God!

....

....

....

....

As I begin my day,
I want to share. . .

....

....

....

....

....

....

....

I am feeling. . .

....

....

....

....

....

....

....

Please infuse my
heart with Your joy!

....

....

....

....

....

Help me to accomplish. . .

....

....

....

....

Thank You for. . .

....

....

....

....

....

....

I am fully giving these worries and concerns to You. . .

....

....

....

....

Other things I need You to know, God. . .

....

....

....

....

Thank You, Father, for hearing my prayers. *Amen.*

My heart says of you, "Seek his face!"
Your face, LORD, I will seek.
PSALM 27:8 NIV

Date: ....

Good morning, God!

....
....
....
....
....

As I begin my day,
I want to share. . .

....
....
....
....
....
....
....

I am feeling. . .

....
....
....
....
....
....
....

Please infuse my
heart with Your joy!

....
....
....
....
....

Help me to accomplish. . .

....

....

....

....

Thank You for. . .

....

....

....

....

....

....

I am fully giving these
worries and concerns to You. . .

....

....

....

....

Other things I need You to know, God. . .

....

....

....

....

Thank You, Father, for hearing my prayers. Amen.

Why not help us make a fresh start—a resurrection life?
Then your people will laugh and sing! Show us how
much you love us, GOD! Give us the salvation we need!
PSALM 85:6–7 MSG

Date: ....

Good morning, God!

....

....

....

....

....

As I begin my day,
I want to share. . .

....

....

....

....

....

....

....

I am feeling. . .

....

....

....

....

....

....

....

Please infuse my
heart with Your joy!

....

....

....

....

....

Help me to accomplish. . .

....
....
....
....

Thank You for. . .

....
....
....
....
....
....

I am fully giving these worries and concerns to You. . .

....
....
....
....

Other things I need You to know, God. . .

....
....
....
....

Thank You, Father, for hearing my prayers. Amen.

"I have swept away your sins like a cloud.
I have scattered your offenses like the morning mist.
Oh, return to me, for I have paid the price to set you free."
ISAIAH 44:22 NLT

Date: ....

Good morning, God!

....
....
....
....
....

As I begin my day,
I want to share. . .

....
....
....
....
....
....
....

I am feeling. . .

....
....
....
....
....
....
....
....

Please infuse my
heart with Your joy!

....
....
....
....
....

Help me to accomplish. . .

....

....

....

....

Thank You for. . .

....

....

....

....

....

....

I am fully giving these
worries and concerns to You. . .

....

....

....

....

Other things I need You to know, God. . .

....

....

....

....

Thank You, Father, for hearing my prayers. *Amen*.

*Everything that we have—right thinking and
right living, a clean slate and a fresh start—
comes from God by way of Jesus Christ.*
1 CORINTHIANS 1:30 MSG

Date: ....

Good morning, God!

....
....
....
....
....

As I begin my day,
I want to share. . .

....
....
....
....
....
....
....
....

I am feeling. . .

....
....
....
....
....
....
....

Please infuse my
heart with Your joy!

....
....
....
....
....

Help me to accomplish. . .

Thank You for. . .

I am fully giving these worries and concerns to You. . .

Other things I need You to know, God. . .

Thank You, Father, for hearing my prayers. *Amen.*

GOD, I do what you tell me. My soul guards and keeps all your instructions—oh, how much I love them! I follow your directions, abide by your counsel; my life's an open book before you.
PSALM 119:166–168 MSG

Date: ....

Good morning, God!

....
....
....
....
....

As I begin my day,
I want to share. . .

....
....
....
....
....
....
....

I am feeling. . .

....
....
....
....
....
....
....

Please infuse my
heart with Your joy!

....
....
....
....
....

Help me to accomplish. . .

....
....
....
....

Thank You for. . .

....
....
....
....
....
....

I am fully giving these
worries and concerns to You. . .

....
....
....
....

Other things I need You to know, God. . .

....
....
....
....

Thank You, Father, for hearing my prayers. *Amen.*

*But he's already made it plain how to live, what to do,
what GOD is looking for in men and women. It's quite
simple: Do what is fair and just to your neighbor,
be compassionate and loyal in your love, and don't
take yourself too seriously—take God seriously.*
MICAH 6:8 MSG

Date: ....

Good morning, God!

....
....
....
....

As I begin my day,
I want to share. . .

....
....
....
....
....
....
....

I am feeling. . .

....
....
....
....
....
....

Please infuse my
heart with Your joy!

....
....
....
....
....

Help me to accomplish. . .

Thank You for. . .

I am fully giving these worries and concerns to You. . .

Other things I need You to know, God. . .

Thank You, Father, for hearing my prayers. Amen.

Open your mouth and taste, open your eyes and see—
how good GOD is. Blessed are you who run to him.
PSALM 34:8 MSG

Date: ....

Good morning, God!

....
....
....
....
....

As I begin my day,
I want to share. . .

....
....
....
....
....
....
....

I am feeling. . .

....
....
....
....
....
....
....

Please infuse my
heart with Your joy!

....
....
....
....
....

Help me to accomplish. . .

....

....

....

....

Thank You for. . .

....

....

....

....

....

....

I am fully giving these
worries and concerns to You. . .

....

....

....

....

Other things I need You to know, God. . .

....

....

....

....

Thank You, Father, for hearing my prayers. Amen.

If you make a run for God—you won't regret it!
PSALM 2:12 MSG

Date: ....

Good morning, God!

....
....
....
....
....

As I begin my day,
I want to share. . .

....
....
....
....
....
....
....

I am feeling. . .

....
....
....
....
....
....
....

Please infuse my
heart with Your joy!

....
....
....
....
....

Help me to accomplish. . .

....

....

....

....

Thank You for. . .

....

....

....

....

....

....

I am fully giving these
worries and concerns to You. . .

....

....

....

Other things I need You to know, God. . .

....

....

....

....

Thank You, Father, for hearing my prayers. *Amen*.

Enjoy God, cheer when you see him!
PSALM 68:4 MSG

Date: ....

Good morning, God!

....
....
....
....
....

As I begin my day,
I want to share. . .

....
....
....
....
....
....
....

I am feeling. . .

....
....
....
....
....
....
....

Please infuse my
heart with Your joy!

....
....
....
....
....

Help me to accomplish. . .

....

....

....

....

Thank You for. . .

....

....

....

....

....

....

I am fully giving these worries and concerns to You. . .

....

....

....

Other things I need You to know, God. . .

....

....

....

....

Thank You, Father, for hearing my prayers. *Amen.*

Satisfy us each morning with your unfailing love,
so we may sing for joy to the end of our lives.
PSALM 90:14 NLT

Date: ....

Good morning, God!

....
....
....
....
....

As I begin my day,
I want to share. . .

....
....
....
....
....
....
....
....

I am feeling. . .

....
....
....
....
....
....
....

Please infuse my
heart with Your joy!

....
....
....
....
....

Help me to accomplish. . .

Thank You for. . .

I am fully giving these worries and concerns to You. . .

Other things I need You to know, God. . .

Thank You, Father, for hearing my prayers. Amen.

Be generous with me and I'll live a full life; not for a minute will I take my eyes off your road. Open my eyes so I can see what you show me of your miracle-wonders.
PSALM 119:17–18 MSG

Date: ....

Good morning, God!

....
....
....
....

As I begin my day,
I want to share. . .

....
....
....
....
....
....
....

I am feeling. . .

....
....
....
....
....
....

Please infuse my
heart with Your joy!

....
....
....
....
....

Help me to accomplish. . .

....

....

....

....

Thank You for. . .

....

....

....

....

....

....

I am fully giving these
worries and concerns to You. . .

....

....

....

Other things I need You to know, God. . .

....

....

....

....

Thank You, Father, for hearing my prayers. *Amen*.

*Blessed are you who give yourselves over to GOD, turn your
backs on the world's "sure thing," ignore what the world
worships; the world's a huge stockpile of GOD-wonders
and God-thoughts. Nothing and no one compares to you!*

PSALM 40:4–5 MSG

Date: ....

Good morning, God!

....
....
....
....
....

As I begin my day,
I want to share. . .

....
....
....
....
....
....
....

I am feeling. . .

....
....
....
....
....
....
....

Please infuse my
heart with Your joy!

....
....
....
....
....

Help me to accomplish. . .

....

....

....

....

Thank You for. . .

....

....

....

....

....

....

I am fully giving these
worries and concerns to You. . .

....

....

....

....

Other things I need You to know, God. . .

....

....

....

....

Thank You, Father, for hearing my prayers. *Amen.*

Great is his faithfulness; his mercies
begin afresh each morning.
LAMENTATIONS 3:23 NLT

Date: ....

Good morning, God!

....

....

....

....

....

As I begin my day,
I want to share. . .

....

....

....

....

....

....

....

I am feeling. . .

....

....

....

....

....

....

....

Please infuse my
heart with Your joy!

....

....

....

....

....

....

Help me to accomplish. . .

....

....

....

....

Thank You for. . .

....

....

....

....

....

....

I am fully giving these
worries and concerns to You. . .

....

....

....

....

Other things I need You to know, God. . .

....

....

....

....

Thank You, Father, for hearing my prayers. *Amen.*

*The spacious, free life is from GOD, it's also protected
and safe. GOD-strengthened, we're delivered from
evil—when we run to him, he saves us.*
PSALM 37:39–40 MSG

Date: ....

Good morning, God!

....
....
....
....

As I begin my day,
I want to share. . .

....
....
....
....
....
....
....

I am feeling. . .

....
....
....
....
....
....
....

Please infuse my
heart with Your joy!

....
....
....
....
....

Help me to accomplish. . .

....
....
....
....
....

Thank You for. . .

....
....
....
....
....
....

I am fully giving these
worries and concerns to You. . .

....
....
....
....

Other things I need You to know, God. . .

....
....
....
....

Thank You, Father, for hearing my prayers. *Amen.*

*May all who seek you rejoice and be glad
in you; may those who long for your saving
help always say, "The LORD is great!"*
PSALM 40:16 NIV

Date: ....

Good morning, God!

....
....
....
....
....

As I begin my day,
I want to share. . .

....
....
....
....
....
....
....
....

I am feeling. . .

....
....
....
....
....
....
....
....

Please infuse my
heart with Your joy!

....
....
....
....
....

Help me to accomplish. . .

Thank You for. . .

I am fully giving these worries and concerns to You. . .

Other things I need You to know, God. . .

Thank You, Father, for hearing my prayers. *Amen*.

What a God! His road stretches straight and
smooth. Every GOD-direction is road-tested.
Everyone who runs toward him makes it.
PSALM 18:30 MSG

Date: ....

Good morning, God!

....
....
....
....
....

As I begin my day,
I want to share. . .

....
....
....
....
....
....
....

I am feeling. . .

....
....
....
....
....
....
....

Please infuse my
heart with Your joy!

....
....
....
....
....

Help me to accomplish. . .

Thank You for. . .

I am fully giving these worries and concerns to You. . .

Other things I need You to know, God. . .

Thank You, Father, for hearing my prayers. *Amen*.

Live a happy life! Keep your eyes open for God,
watch for his works; be alert for signs of his presence.
PSALM 105:3–4 MSG

Date: ....

Good morning, God!

....
....
....
....
....

As I begin my day,
I want to share. . .

....
....
....
....
....
....
....

I am feeling. . .

....
....
....
....
....
....
....

Please infuse my
heart with Your joy!

....
....
....
....
....

Help me to accomplish. . .

....
....
....
....

Thank You for. . .

....
....
....
....
....
....

I am fully giving these
worries and concerns to You. . .

....
....
....

Other things I need You to know, God. . .

....
....
....
....

Thank You, Father, for hearing my prayers. *Amen*.

*Your strength will be renewed
each day like the morning dew.*
PSALM 110:3 NLT

Date: ....

Good morning, God!

....
....
....
....
....

As I begin my day,
I want to share. . .

....
....
....
....
....
....
....

I am feeling. . .

....
....
....
....
....
....
....

Please infuse my
heart with Your joy!

....
....
....
....
....

Help me to accomplish. . .

....

....

....

....

Thank You for. . .

....

....

....

....

....

....

I am fully giving these worries and concerns to You. . .

....

....

....

....

Other things I need You to know, God. . .

....

....

....

....

Thank You, Father, for hearing my prayers. *Amen.*

Open up before God, keep nothing back; he'll do whatever needs to be done: He'll validate your life in the clear light of day and stamp you with approval at high noon.
PSALM 37:5–6 MSG

Date: ....

Good morning, God!

....
....
....
....
....

As I begin my day,
I want to share. . .

....
....
....
....
....
....
....

I am feeling. . .

....
....
....
....
....
....
....

Please infuse my
heart with Your joy!

....
....
....
....
....

Help me to accomplish. . .

....

....

....

....

Thank You for. . .

....

....

....

....

....

I am fully giving these
worries and concerns to You. . .

....

....

....

....

Other things I need You to know, God. . .

....

....

....

....

Thank You, Father, for hearing my prayers. *Amen.*

*"Because of God's tender mercy, the morning
light from heaven is about to break upon us."*
LUKE 1:78 NLT

Date: ....

Good morning, God!

....
....
....
....
....

As I begin my day,
I want to share. . .

....
....
....
....
....
....
....

I am feeling. . .

....
....
....
....
....
....
....

Please infuse my
heart with Your joy!

....
....
....
....
....

Help me to accomplish. . .

....

....

....

....

Thank You for. . .

....

....

....

....

....

....

I am fully giving these
worries and concerns to You. . .

....

....

....

....

Other things I need You to know, God. . .

....

....

....

....

Thank You, Father, for hearing my prayers. *Amen.*

*Keep me safe, O God, I've run for dear
life to you. I say to GOD, "Be my Lord!"
Without you, nothing makes sense.*
PSALM 16:1–2 MSG

Date: ....

Good morning, God!

....
....
....
....
....

As I begin my day,
I want to share. . .

....
....
....
....
....
....
....

I am feeling. . .

....
....
....
....
....
....
....
....

Please infuse my
heart with Your joy!

....
....
....
....
....

Help me to accomplish. . .

Thank You for. . .

I am fully giving these worries and concerns to You. . .

Other things I need You to know, God. . .

Thank You, Father, for hearing my prayers. *Amen.*

Even though on the outside it often looks like things are falling apart on us, on the inside, where God is making new life, not a day goes by without his unfolding grace.
2 CORINTHIANS 4:16–17 MSG

Date: ....

Good morning, God!

....
....
....
....
....

As I begin my day,
I want to share. . .

....
....
....
....
....
....
....

I am feeling. . .

....
....
....
....
....
....
....
....

Please infuse my
heart with Your joy!

....
....
....
....
....
....

Help me to accomplish. . .

....

....

....

....

Thank You for. . .

....

....

....

....

....

....

I am fully giving these worries and concerns to You. . .

....

....

....

....

Other things I need You to know, God. . .

....

....

....

....

Thank You, Father, for hearing my prayers. *Amen.*

*I remain confident of this: I will see the
goodness of the LORD in the land of the living.*
PSALM 27:13 NIV

Date: ....

Good morning, God!

....
....
....
....
....

As I begin my day,
I want to share. . .

....
....
....
....
....
....
....

I am feeling. . .

....
....
....
....
....
....
....

Please infuse my
heart with Your joy!

....
....
....
....
....

Help me to accomplish. . .

Thank You for. . .

I am fully giving these worries and concerns to You. . .

Other things I need You to know, God. . .

Thank You, Father, for hearing my prayers. *Amen.*

You've always given me breathing room, a place to get away from it all, a lifetime pass to your safehouse, an open invitation as your guest. You've always taken me seriously, God, made me welcome among those who know and love you.

PSALM 61:3–5 MSG

Date: ....

Good morning, God!

....
....
....
....
....

As I begin my day,
I want to share. . .

....
....
....
....
....
....
....
....

I am feeling. . .

....
....
....
....
....
....
....
....

Please infuse my
heart with Your joy!

....
....
....
....
....

Help me to accomplish. . .

....

....

....

....

Thank You for. . .

....

....

....

....

....

I am fully giving these worries and concerns to You. . .

....

....

....

....

Other things I need You to know, God. . .

....

....

....

....

Thank You, Father, for hearing my prayers. *Amen.*

"I, Jesus, have sent my angel to give you this message for the churches. I am both the source of David and the heir to his throne. I am the bright morning star."
REVELATION 22:16 NLT

DISCOVER MORE FAITH MAPS
FOR THE ENTIRE FAMILY. . .

The Prayer Map for Men
978-1-64352-438-2

The Prayer Map for Boys
978-1-68322-558-4

The Prayer Map for Women
978-1-68322-557-7

The Prayer Map for Teens
978-1-68322-556-0

The Prayer Map for Girls
978-1-68322-559-1

The Prayer Map for Teen Girls
978-1-63609-803-6

These purposeful prayer journals are a fun and creative way to more fully experience the power of prayer. Each page guides you to write out thoughts, ideas, and lists. . .creating a specific "map" for you to follow as you talk to God. Each map includes a spot to record the date, so you can look back on your prayers and see how God has worked in your life. *The Prayer Map* will not only encourage you to spend time talking with God about the things that matter most. . .it will also help you build a healthy spiritual habit of continual prayer for life!

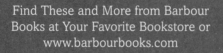